Soon and Very Soon

By Leland Roebke

Evidence indicates that...
Two major events are soon to take place
that will affect every individual
on Planet Earth.

Copyright ©2022 by Leland Roebke

All rights reserved. This book or any portion thereof may not be reproduced or used in any manner without the express written permission of the author except for the use of brief quotations in a book review.

ISBN: 978-1-949565-76-8

Printed in the U.S.A. by
Smith Printing, LLC
Ramsey, MN 55303
(800) 416-9099 • www.smithprinting.com
Printed in the United States of America.

Front Cover Photo Credit:
Steve Brzezinski/JC Creations

All scriptures quoted are from the
New King James version.

The writer takes no responsibility for the accuracy of the quotes or probabilities nor any guarantees that the content is or will remain accurate or appropriate.

Soon and Very Soon?.....
So what is the Evidence?

There seems to be a unanimous agreement amongst most people that the world as we know it today is a vastly different place to live than it was even a few years ago. Some of that 'different' could be good and some likely is, but it seems that most of the change for most of the people falls into the category of 'not so good'. Is it a truism or is it a fact that when compared to 'before', life today is more difficult, more different, confusing, unfriendly, even weird, and all too often life is simply hard to deal with? Then add to that another truism: 'things don't seem to be getting better, but actually are getting yet more difficult.' There are many reasons for the difficulties, but let us not forget Covid 19,…. Yikes. Covid changed everything everywhere. So, whatever the reasons, here we are, so desiring that things could be as they once were.

In addition to the dilemmas of the day, a further disturbing reality is the open and extremely destructive war between Russia and Ukraine (not really a war, but an invasion by a super power), and we find things internationally in crisis as well. What will be the worldwide consequences upon the economies and the sustaining of life's needs, for the people of the world, once the full impact of this invasion is realized? I understand that these words are quite negative, but the reality is: this is where we are in the world of our day. Is there nowhere to escape, or avoid the harsh realities of life today that seem to be everywhere, affecting virtually everyone?

There are many people, churches, ministries, and geopolitical/social organizations which believe we live in the closing days of recorded history. The 'New Green Deal' adherents believe that climate change is creating environmental conditions and severe weather with the resulting combination making life universally so unlivable that the world has only a limited number of years (12 years according to some) before the climate changes will make life as we know it very difficult or impossible. Look at the mad rush that has been made to get the world into renewable energy by the year 2050 or before. Consider the mad rush by auto manufacturers and states like California to commit fully to EV's by 2035! Many climatologists believe that the world does not have 30 years to make the necessary adjustments. What then? Still others believe that the present world population of 8 billion will threaten the food, fresh water supplies and natural resources to the point that the peoples of the world will simply run out of the necessities of life and that the shortages and the resulting diseases will create the demise of millions.

The God of the Bible has also made many statements regarding the 'End of the Age' and has made many predictions regarding what the times 'just before the end' would be like. The Bible has not only made statements about the times on earth during those 'End of Days', but in addition has provided 'sign posts' or 'identifiers' so the observer living at that time could see certain prophesied events taking place, right before their eyes. These 'written beforehand items' are called prophecies and the Bible is abundant with events that have already been fulfilled and some are about the times in which we live. About 30% of the Bible is prophetic and hundreds of the Bible's prophecies deal with the times of the 'End'. If these prophecies can be proven to be accurate, then they become strong, even irrefutable evidences that the prophetic words of the Bible are in fact true. Hundreds and even thousands of years ago God made references regarding many future times and events and the fulfillment of those prophecies have been proven to be absolutely accurate. We are going to take a look at some of the 'prophetic utterances' regarding the Biblical accounts about the 'Time of the End'. God was willing to risk His reputation by telling those who are alive at the 'End of the Age, what the 'End of the Age' times would look like.

In the coming pages we will consider some of the many Biblical prophetic announcements about things and events regarding the 'End of Days'. These prophetic words have come to be fulfilled during a very short period of time, a time during which we are alive (this was written in the summer of 2022).

Let me define a few terms/events that will be mentioned:

The Rapture: A soon coming event that will extract all Believers in Jesus Christ from the very face of the Earth. A prophetic event that will 'Rescue the Believers alive' and usher them to Heaven before the terrible events of the Tribulation Period (Bible's Book of Revelation) begin to take place on planet Earth.

The Tribulation Period: A horrible seven year period that takes place on Earth soon after the Rapture of the Church. It will feature horrific times of existence and the control and leadership of an Evil Individual as described in Revelation Ch 6-18.

Before dealing with the reality of the many Biblical prophecies regarding the times in which we live, allow me to go back to a most critical period of time, when Jesus Christ came into the world as the physical manifestation of God/Man on Earth. Let us acknowledge that all of history is date connected to the birthdate of Jesus Christ.

About 30 years after Jesus was born, He was crucified, buried and then rose again just as the Old Testament scriptures said He would. Jesus Christ thereby became the Savior of the World. The death of Jesus Christ on a cross was to bear the penalty for the sins of world. Jesus became the Savior for all who would accept His sacrifice as if He had died for each of us individually. This event, where Jesus became the Savior of the World, is considered the very most important happening ever, in the history of everything and anything. God sent His Son Jesus to Earth where He lived, died and was then resurrected to accomplish the perfect sacrifice for the punishment of the sins of mankind, thus the sins of each individual and to thereby defeat death. Eternity with God is the free gift of God in that it can be had by each of us by acknowledging our sinful state before The All Holy God and accepting the sacrifice of Jesus Christ on our behalf. There will be more on this at the end of this book. What is at hand here and the message of 'Soon and Very Soon' is to accept the Free Gift of God and be Raptured… or deny that Free Gift and experience the ravages of the Tribulation Period and perhaps eternal Hell as well. This is what this writing is all about.

God is not done with world events. God has a plan and His ultimate plan will not be frustrated, but will come to fruition as He has said. Many believe that the future of mankind, not far in the distance, is about to change dramatically. For some it will be marvelous and for others it will be catastrophic. To repeat, the two things that are on the near horizon that will dramatically change life on earth are: 1. the Rapture of the Church, or taking up or away physically the believers in Jesus Christ from the Earth, and 2. the 7 year Tribulation Period as described in the Book of Revelation, (Chapters 6-18). This Tribulation Period (7 years in duration) will severely and adversely affect every man, woman, and child who was not Raptured…. Stay with me and believe me when I say that much has been written in the Bible about these events. There are many current happenings that describe the uniqueness of our time in history (the modern era) that were prophesied hundreds and even thousands of years ago. These prophetic fulfillments create tremendous evidence that the other words of the Bible must be true as well.

You may be asking 'Why Now' does the subject of the Rapture and the Tribulation seem to be so important or pertinent in today's world, when in the past there was not too much attention given to these 'Last Days' events. Good question. Let me try to answer it. In most stages of life and history there are proper times to do 'due diligence.' God has a timetable and never wants us to be unaware or unprepared. In Noah's time there was a 100 year warning to the world regarding the need to repent, or to be 'Left Behind'. 100 years later the doors closed on the Ark and the tragedy was underway. Same today? There were many centuries between the Fall and the Flood but the warning did not come until it was pertinent to the time of its inception. Timing must be pertinent to the time of the event or it is simply a discussion that has no direct application. Proper timing is a truism, no matter the situation. The proper time to understand the coming events discussed in this book is now, not later because the events of the Rapture & the Tribulation are just around the corner, perhaps today. That makes this subject even more pertinent regarding its importance to you in order for you to have the correct understandings regarding these future events and their effect upon you and those you love.

The reason for the writing of 'Soon and Very Soon' is to allow the reader the opportunity to become aware of some of the Biblical prophecies about the uniqueness of our present age. The current events and inventions that are unique to the times of today only, our modern era, and the fact that all of these prophecies have been fulfilled at the same time in history (convergence) makes these times unusual to say the least. This text is designed to help one see that the following 20+ prophetic fulfillments are so unique and timely that it is statistically impossible to consider their convergence as a coincidence. You, as the reader of 'Soon and Very Soon' are the one who gets to consider whether or not these 'historically unique happenings' are really prophetic fulfillments or just coincidences. If you conclude that these events are unique to our time and that the Bible is therefore true and accurate on these items, should you not consider that the other things the Bible says about eternal matters must be considered true as well?

Before dealing with the evidences, let's consider the attitude that the Scriptures call for regarding this subject. Whether the reader is an atheist, agnostic, sceptic, believer, or an occasional 'church goer', listed below are some attitudes that the reader should have in order to see the truth of what is being considered. According to the Bible the readers would be best equipped if they would consider the 'prophecies' from these perspectives:

- Looking for the Blessed Hope, the Appearing of our Great God and Savior.
  Titus 2:23
- Anxiously, eagerly awaiting.
  1 Cor.1:17

- Eagerly waiting for the Savior.
Phil.3:20-21
- He is coming – Appearing. Watch your life. Col.1:9
- Comfort one another – Salvation awaits.
I Thess. 5:9-11
- He shall be revealed – our Hope.
I John 3:2-3
- Eagerly waiting for the Redemption of our Body. Rom. 8:23
- Wait for His Son from Heaven to deliver us. I Thess. 1:10
- Watch and be sober – no sleeping.
I Thess. 5:6

What has God told the readers of the Scriptures regarding the Rapture, or the 'Catching Away':

- I do not want you to be ignorant or uniformed regarding those who have fallen asleep. I Thess.4:13-18
- See, I have told you beforehand.
Matt. 24:25

- The prophetic Word is confirmed & we need to heed it as a light that shines in a dark place II Peter 1:19

- Paul tells the story of the sequence of current events I Cor. 15:51-54
- I will come again and receive you to Myself, John 14:3
- The Last Day prophetic events will be like labor pains, closer and more intense and then repeat, but worse.

I Thess. 5:3
Matt 24:8

Future events (End Time scenarios, prophecies) have been told beforehand, pre written by the God of the Bible. They are essential writings in order for the Church and everyone else watching to know, in order to understand what is going to happen at some point in the future. The writings are particularly relevant for those that are living on the Earth when the prophecies are taking place; that they may know and understand the times in which they live. Isaiah 46:9-10 tells us that God knows the end from the beginning, "I can tell you the future exactly". Regarding the future, one current author put it this way: 'For those of you that live during the 'Days of the End'… either know the Words of God and escape…or get your life rocked and terrified'. God's word is to be trusted from the beginning to the end, for it is positively accurate, we can know absolutely. Prophecy is a fact. Anchor yourself in it as you see the 'Day' approaching. By applying the prophetic Word of God to the 'Modern Era Times' in which we live, we can observe these times for what they are and be prepared… and escape the prophesied horror of The Tribulation Period. Jesus Christ is coming again and for some the joy of eternity awaits them… and for many more, hell on earth will be the best it ever gets.

In a book titled 'The Math of Jesus', author Stephen M. Bauer gives the probability of just 40 correct fulfillments out of the 300 prophecies recorded in the Bible regarding Jesus Christ and His 1st coming to earth. The 300 prophecies regarding the 1st coming of Jesus to earth dealt with items such as where He would be born, the fact that He would go to Egypt as a child, the name of the village where He would grow up, how He would die, and about 290 other descriptions of His life. These prophecies were written hundreds of years before Jesus was even born. The combined probability of 40 of the 300 prophecies happening by one person at one particular time in history is 1×10^{136} That is 1 followed by 136 zeros. 1 in 1 is a fact, 1 in 2 is a 50% probability, 1 in 100 is a 1% probability, and 1 in 1000 is 'forget it.' Well, to say it again, the probability of Jesus fulfilling just 40 of the 300 prophecies regarding His 1st coming to earth is 1 in 1 followed by 136 zeros. 1 in 1 followed by 50 zeros is considered by statisticians to be an impossible probability, instead it is simply a fact. The conclusion: except for the reality that these Biblical prophesies were from the Omniscient God who spoke to the prophets of the Old Testament, who then wrote as God instructed, there is no other explanation. The remaining bulk of this book is about pre written Biblical prophecies that have come to be fulfilled in 'recent days.' What needs to be considered is whether these fulfilled prophesied events are coincidences of major proportion or instead the fulfillment of previously written Biblical prophetic utterances. Like in the example shown above there seems to be no possibility of these events all happening at the 'same time' in history being coincidences….more of the undeniable reality that the happenings that will be shown, are the result of God speaking to prophets and the prophets writing for our benefit and then the prophetic words coming to pass.

The book of Matthew, chapter 24 is called the 'Olivet Discourse' and is one of the most important references to 'End Time or Last Days' utterances…. It is best understood when divided into the following 3 sections:

> To all but particularly to & about the nation of Israel……. Verses 4-31
>
> To all but particularly to & about Israel and the Church…. Verses 32-35
>
> To all but particularly to & about the Church………Verses 36-51

The 'Convergence of End Time Events', mentioned by Jesus in Matt. 24:33 & Luke 21:38 are critically important and give incredible evidence to the subject at hand. The apostle Luke wrote: 'When these things begin to happen (prophecies fulfilled), look up and lift up your heads, because your redemption (the Rapture of the Church) draws near'. There will be a time (like now) in history when many historically mind shattering events and inventions will happen in the shadows of each other, things that can easily be traced to biblical prophecy. As will be shown, these fulfillments have all happened during the same time in world history (convergence). In Soon and Very soon are listed some 20+ 'Convergence End time events and inventions'. I would imagine that with a bit more study, that number could be substantially increased but that would simply add to the probability of these fulfillments being facts. I believe we will see that such is already the case. There are billions of people living on the earth during these Last Days that can observe the events and billions that are actually involved in the prophetic happenings by means of participation or employment. Consider the possibility of all of these 20+ signs happening at the same time in one small period of history (convergence)… beyond probability.

All of the prophetic events that are mentioned in this book started 150 to 170 years ago and have had their needed fulfillment by now or are in the process of completing it.

- 150 years means that all of the prophetic signs mentioned herein happened within 2.5% of the historical period of recorded history to today. The beginning of recorded history is about 6000 years ago.

- For the signs to be fulfilled within 100 years means they were fulfilled in the limits of 1.7% of recorded history.

- For signs to be fulfilled within 50 years means they were fulfilled in the limits of .8% of recorded history.

- This simply means that the End Time prophecies that we will consider, have happened, from beginning (1850 or later) to today, or within 2.5% of the time of recorded history. There is a building of the process(es) of prophecies that require time of maturing before the full application can be applied (computer industry, electricity, automobiles, or medical as examples). Each has been around for decades, but today they are beyond the wildest imagination compared to any applications possible of when each started. Today each of these fulfilled prophecies is critical to life as we know it and for billions of people… just coincidences?

- The fulfillment of these many prophecies happening in one short period of time, during what seems to be at the 'End of Time' is beyond probability. Their coming together to create a historical woven modernization miracle and to do so during a tight specific time period is a fact: and the reality that they are prophetic fulfillments as well is undeniable. That is a Wow.

As we will see, all of the prophetic signs we are considering started about 1850 or later and intensified and grew into the 1960's and then into what they have become today. Many have grown exponentially, beyond whatever could have been imagined while others have perhaps even reached their full-blown potential (automobiles and plugged freeways). We are forced to do things electronically that in the past were simply a phone call or a paper and pencil requirement. Today an individual must be proficient on a computer and cell phone, create and use passwords and user names (and change them every 90 days). We are forced to operate computerized automobiles designed by Whiz Kid engineers, and soon will have to deal with the effects of artificial intelligence. Yikes. Let's take a look at some of the Biblical prophetic utterances unique to our Day and their recent fulfillments. Do these fulfillments overwhelmingly indicate that these days in which we live, are in fact the 'Last Days' as described by the Bible:

MEN SHALL GO TO AND FRO….

170 years ago it was common for a person not to travel more than 40 miles from where they were born…in their entire lifetime. Today millions of people are members of the 'Million Mile' club: a million miles of travel in their lifetime. The average American travels 14,263 miles each year. Today, worldwide, there are over 8 billion cars, buses, planes, trucks, and motor cycles that transport people and goods, some even into space. Men shall go 'to and fro' is a prophetic statement that is being fulfilled today with profound consequences, happening at a precise time in history. This is quite a prophetic announcement given to us by the angel Gabriel and the prophet Daniel, that there would come a time when people worldwide would travel extensively and that this phenomenon would take place at the Time of the End.

Daniel 12:4

KNOWLEDGE SHALL INCREASE...

About 2600 years ago the Angel Gabriel told Daniel the Prophet to close the Book until 'The Time of the End' and then simply said: 'Knowledge shall Increase'. That could be interpreted as: at the time of the 'End', there will be a significant increase in knowledge. Ever consider the fact that your cell phone is small enough to fit in your pocket and yet it is an encyclopedia, a multiple communication device, a map, a weather forecaster, a camera, and a hundred other features? The computer, electricity, automobile, airplanes, organ transplants, & trips to space are additional examples and are yet only a few of the volumes of examples that could be used regarding the reality of 'Knowledge Increasing'.

As you read this book further you will see how critical today's technology is to the fulfillment of many of the prophecies that we will look at. Also, consider that 'it' all started with this exponential fulfillment regarding knowledge increasing. Virtually every prophetic fulfillment that we will consider requires the development of knowledge (mechanical/electrical/technology of some consequence) in order for the prophetic utterance to become a reality.

Daniel 12:4

ISRAEL BECOMES A NATION…

The people of Israel were scattered to the four corners of the world after the dispersion of 70 AD and remained that way until they received Nationhood in 1948. The restoration of the nation of Israel as a separate and sovereign people is considered the 'Stand Out' of all Last Days prophecies. Dry bones became functional bodies occupying the Land of Israel once again, happening just as the Bible said it would. Israel is a nation of less than 10 million people, yet it is an international leader in virtually every segment of daily life, including medicine, agriculture, weapons, technology, gas & oil production, & humanitarian efforts. Israel's contribution to the world is noble to say the least.

The prophecies regarding Israel in the final days are precise – about a people, the Apple of God's Eye, a people who were, then were not, and now they are, just as God said they would be. Never in all of history has such ever taken place. When a people or a culture have been removed or dispersed, they are gone, never to have prominence again. Not so with Israel. They are back bigger and more prominent than ever.

Ezekiel Ch. 36-38
Matthew Ch. 24

Allow me to give a more detailed summary of the restoration of the Nation of Israel to its present status:

The restoration of the nation of Israel to its present state from what it was even 100 years ago is nothing short of a spectacular prophetic miracle. Think of it, a recognized nation of people in 70 AD, internationally scattered and then 2000 years later spectacularly returned to their homeland to become a recognized and internationally powerful nation. About 2000 years ago Jesus prophesied in Matthew 24:2 that Jerusalem would be sieged, not one stone left upon another. Some 40 years after that prophecy (70 AD) Jerusalem was ravaged by the Romans, over 1 million Jews were killed and the remainder of the Jews in Jerusalem were scattered to the four corners of the known world of that day. From 70 AD until the rebirth of Israel (5/14/48) the land was inhabited by a limited number of people(s) and was considered by those that were familiar with the area as a partially occupied neglected wasteland. The region came under the sway of various empires, ethnic groups, and religions, including Judaism, Sarmatianism, Christianity, Islam, and others.

The late 19th century saw the rise of Zionism (a movement of Jews realizing the need to again become a 'people' occupying the land that God gave to them centuries before). With the fall of the Ottoman Empire in the early 20th century it was declared that Great Britain would take on the responsibility of guiding the future of the Zionists. In 1917 the Belfour Declaration was signed and it stated that the British government would do everything in its power to create a Jewish State in the Holy Land. This endorsement in part led to a huge surge in Jewish migration to the Holy Land in the decade immediately following WWII. British control lasted from 1923 to 1948 during which the Brits were challenged to allow the Jews living in the land to be self-governing, which the Jews did. Also, the loss of some 6 million Jews during the Holocaust gave the Jews world support regarding their demands for national sovereignty. Israel's establishment national sovereignty. Israel's establishment as an independent sovereign state was officially declared in Tel Aviv on Friday May 14, 1948 and…. Israel was immediately attacked and invaded by armies of five Arab nations. Outnumbered badly, yet the newly formed nation managed to prevail after 15 months of war.

More wars and conflicts were and are a part of the history of Israel, but today they are a great nation, respected by friend and foe. Today there are about 9.5 million Israelis in Israel of which about 75% are Jews.

The number of Biblical references that prophecy that Israel would again one day be a great nation are many. Here are a few that you could reference, prophecies that were spoken thousands of years ago and prophecies about Israel that today have come to pass…right before our eyes. Beyond comprehension.

> Jeremiah 30:1-2, 31:8-10
> Isaiah 11:12, 27:2-6,
> Ezekiel Ch. 37.
> Luke 21:24 (fall of Jerusalem)

1984…… THE BOOK, THE MOVIE, THE TRUISM, THE REALITY…

We are in a time today where every person in the world can be known, controlled & manipulated. Advanced computer technology has the hardware to know and control virtually every person in the world. Where does artificial intelligence fit into all of this; it is real and functioning…. and frightening? Motion and face recognition is here and who knows what more is in the near future. How close are we to becoming cashless?… according to many, very close, and what kind of further control might that implement? These technologies are recent by any terms and will be required for the application of the absolute control of all persons in the world during the Tribulation Period.

May I encourage you to take a few minutes to read Revelation chapter 13 and consider how relevant it is in the details of the world facing us today… and then consider that these historical prophetic words were penned 2000 years ago.

Revelation 13:15-17

LAWLESSNESS WILL ABOUND…

When did it really start?… Some say Obama with his statements that he will change the United States unalterably. I believe the change really started, in a way that could be seen and measured, with the incident of George Floyd. The riots, destruction, and lawlessness that ensued in Minneapolis and other cities and places all over the world seemed to give license to many, making it fashionable and reasonable to endorse a whole 'other' way of life and behaving. It is obvious that since that time in June of 2020 there has become an evident disregard for law and order, police and simple respect, with a resulting 'Free Reign' of Lawlessness…Just as Jesus said it would be near the time of His return. Murder in America was up 29% in 2020 compared to 2019. The Apostle Paul told us that in the 'Latter Days' there would be 'perilous times', meaning dangerous to people and property…and evil and demonic as well. Cities and larger towns are trying to create ways to reduce the violence, but since lawlessness is primarily a moral and ethical problem, and the current reality is that morality and ethics are not 'in vogue' nor taught, therefore most attempted solutions will be vain efforts. Either societies become police states with severe punishment for disobedience in order to 'force' correct behavior or start to deal with the heart of individuals to create a self disciplined citizen. We know the latter will not be happening (teaching morals and ethics to the masses) so we should be able to determine what the future will be regarding 'lawlessness'… get used to it.

Is it coincidence that with one incident on one day in 2020 it seems that the world changed and the prophecy of Jesus in Matthew 24 had a more precise beginning. 'Lawlessness will Abound' seems to be tied to a date and that just happened to be at the same time in history as so many other fulfilled prophetic statements are being fulfilled, during the same season.

Matt. 24:12
II Tim. 3:1

A LIST OF LAST DAY GRIEVANCES, THE WAY IT WILL BE IN THOSE LAST DAYS…

The Apostle Paul alerts his readers to the coming times when selfish, unkind, unfriendly, vicious, and even brutal attitudes and behaviors will be prevalent…a time Paul refers to as 'The last Days'. It is a time during which the Biblical World View will not be recognized or used by the majority, or tolerated and will even be abandoned by many, if not most. Then Paul lists many of the resulting consequences for those that are living during that time. Sounds like reading the newspaper or watching the evening news. Take a look at II Timothy 3:1-9 and see what you think.

Dr. David Reagan, in a recent article summarized this passage as:
1. Love of self is Humanism.
2. Love of money is Materialism.
3. Love of pleasure is Hedonism.
4. The result is Nihilism which is a fancy word for Despair. The word really

describes the denial or rejection of any customary belief in morality, ethics, or religion. This list of attitudes, behaviors, and activities is very descriptive of life for multitudes in the western world of today.

It is 'in your face' evident, that in a short period of history, attitudes and behaviors have changed radically, just as the Apostle proclaimed they would. Another example of a prophetic fulfillment that now affects the lives of literally everyone.

II Timothy 3:1-9

THE TWO WITNESSES SEEN BY THE WORLD…

In the book of Revelation there is the narrative about Two Witnesses that will be near the temple gate in Old Jerusalem and they will be there for the 1st half of the 7 year Tribulation Period. The Scriptures say that these Two Witnesses will be viewed by the whole world during their 3 ½ years in Jerusalem. Biblical scholars of the past had no idea how such a worldwide observance could ever be possible. 'Surely this shall never be'. God redeemed Himself regarding the truth of these prophetic words with the marvels of Satellite Television and later the Cell Phone and Internet. Today this is a part of our now common 'Increased knowledge' and the timing is impeccable.

Is it just a coincidence or is it prophetic that Satellite Television and Cell Phone technology would come to be just in time for this prophetic pageant to be able to be seen by the whole world? Quite astounding!

Revelation 11:9

LOVERS OF PLEASURE RATHER THAN LOVERS OF GOD…

The Outdoor Recreation Industry did not even exist in 1900…today the industry is worth about $850 billion per year and employs about 6.1 million people. Recreation in our world is a source of pleasure, physical activity, health, social interaction, and even addiction. As a result, recreation as it is played out today, is a major consumer of money, energy, and time on the part of the many that participate. What about the other forms of recreation available in our world? God has so much competition today. It is true that today much of the world thinks of the need to have 'fun' doing almost everything and anything. Even at the work place, employees want to work where they will have 'fun'. Really?

An industry that did not even exist a century ago, now occupies the time, talent, and resources of millions (billions?) of people. Is this industry the result of our becoming more civilized and modern, or is the result tied to Biblical Prophecy? Either way it certainly is prophetic and fulfilled.

II Timothy 3:4

MANY WILL COME IN MY NAME, CLAIMING TO BE THE CHRIST...

In Matthew 24:3-5 Jesus predicts that at the 'End of the Age' there would be many false Christs that would appear and deceive many. The same text is recorded in Luke chapter 21 and there the subject of false Christ's is expressed as 'many will come in My name, saying, 'I am He'. Many have come to believe this is the recent decline or influence of the Church, but I believe we must consider instead that the recent advancement of the cults would be the proper interpretation. Many Churches and denominations have 'gone liberal' and allowed other untruths, but I know of none that have claimed another or false Christ. Consider these start dates for the major cults of the world:

    Mormons: 1839
    Jehovah's Witnesses: 1870's
    New Age: 1960's
    Moonies: 1954
    Christian Science: 1875
    Scientology: 1950's

All of these cults have had their start within the last 3% of recorded history and yet were mentioned by Jesus 2000 years ago as a sign of His Coming again! The Mormon church (a cult that would like to be mainstreamed with Christianity) is the fastest growing religious organization in the world.

The definition of a cult is a religion that is unorthodox in its teaching, one that denies essential truths, or defines itself by its unusual religious, spiritual, or philosophical beliefs or rituals. In Biblical terms it would be defined as a group that denies one or more of the fundamental Biblical truths.

Matthew 24:3-5
Luke 21:7-8

MURDER, AMORAL SEX, THEFTS, DRUGS…

The four major crimes during the time of the Tribulation will be Murder, Amoral Sex, Thefts and Drugs. …(Sorceries is the common word used in the bible to describe the 4th crime in Revelation 9:21. It actually means druggings (medicinal or mind altering), coming from the Greek word pharmakeia from which the English word pharmaceuticals is derived). These are the major crimes of today and have been the four 'majors' for only about the past 60 years. When drugs entered the scene (1960 or so), the use and sale of drugs became a crime in and of itself. In addition, the result of the drug scene was that all other crimes increased even yet further. I grew up in a time when drugs and drug abuse was an unknown… not so today. Today the trafficking and abuse of drugs in the USA affects nearly all aspects of our daily lives. The economic cost alone is staggering, estimated at over $250 billion annually. The damage caused by drug abuse and addiction is reflected in countless lost lives, destruction of families and individuals, an overburdened justice system, and a strained health care system. Additionally, there is lost productivity, environmental destruction and a very negative impact on all aspects of every society. Drugs are a plight of the worse nature placed upon the modern world, driven by personal choice and resulting in horrific addictions and untold trauma. Is it just coincidental that when the Apostle John penned the book of Revelation in about 100 AD, he wrote that drugs and the resulting individual and social impact would be devastating? The Apostle John, 2000 years ago, was inspired to write just a few words about a subject that would overwhelm the world of the 'End Times'… without any understanding of how devastating the impact of that 4th major crime would be.

It is quite evident that this recent 4th major crime is a most convincing fulfilled prophecy, one that is having devastating consequences upon the whole world. It is one of those 'in your face every day' prophetic events. This fulfillment seems so improbable that perhaps it is enough for one to proclaim that Biblical prophecy is true and needs to be heeded and considered fully. The 'Drugs' (4th major crime) prophecy was written 2000 years ago and started happening some 60 years ago and is culture changing today.

Revelation 9:21

WARS AND RUMORS OF WARS...

Interesting that the only world wars ever to take place in history did so during the 20th century. In today's world, there are wars and skirmishes going on always and some of them are and have been very serious. As of this writing there are 40 wars and skirmishes in the world and at the top is the major war Russia has imposed upon Ukraine, today in full bloom. More people died as the result of wars during the 20th century than all previous centuries combined. The number of war victims (dead) during the 20th century is estimated at 160 million. The real interpretation of some of the words used by Jesus would be translated as 'ethnic wars' (of which in recent history there have been many) and in addition many of the more recent wars are where dictators killed their own people. During the 20th and 21st centuries millions upon millions of people died fighting their 'neighbors' and millions more died at the hands of their political leaders.

That's not all Jesus had to say about war. He also said there would be rumors of wars. Let's look at the list of rumors of wars that are prevalent at the time of this writing:

    Russia and NATO nations & USA?
    China and Taiwan
    China and USA
    Iran and USA (great Satan) & Israel (little Satan)
    Russia and Israel
    North Korea and South Korea & the USA?
    War of Gog and Magog - Israel and an Arab confederation

Let's agree that any war or threat of war in this age is a threat to world security and potentially a dangerous confrontation.

For Jesus to predict 2000 years ago that life would be as we find it today is quite astounding, is it not? If Jesus was/is so very accurate in this arena, should we not pay attention to the other things He said as well. Seems reasonable and even compelling!

                        24:6-7Matthew

PESTILANCE…

Viruses are a part of the diseases as described in the word 'pestilence'. Do we need to go over the two terrible years during which the lives of virtually every human on earth were disrupted and forever changed due to a virus. Those two years were called by one TV program review as: 'The two years that changed the world'. In all of world history there have been only two other events that have affected every single person alive in the entire world at the same time: 1. the Flood, and 2. the destruction of the Tower of Babel. Also, the Covid 19 mandates took the world perilously close to fulfilling the Revelation 13:16-17: 'Individual control' prophecy, via a mark (of the Beast) or a vaccine pass card. And… It is likely not over yet.

Matthew 24:7.
Revelation 13:16-17

DO NOT FORSAKE THE ASSEMBLING TOGETHER...AS YOU SEE THE DAY APPROACHING

In Hebrews 10:25, the writer mentions a situation that before Covid was a bit of a mystery. Why the mention of assembling issues regarding the Church and tying them to the 'Time' of the Lord's return? Obviously, something would be going on before the 'Day' arrived and would take down Church attendance. None other but Covid 19. Note the strong message that the writer of Hebrews gives: 'Do Not forsake the assembling together'. Nothing about convenience or health concerns or live streaming. Obviously in God's mind it is critically important for the believers to congregate with each other… the assembling together of the Church is a major issue, even in the midst of a pandemic.

Hebrews 10:25

WEAPONS OF MASS DESTRUCTION…

Twice in the book of Revelation (the Tribulation Period) John reveals that $1/4^{th}$ and then $1/3^{rd}$ of the population of the earth will die (be killed?) and while it could be natural disasters, starvation, disease, chemical warfare…or in today's world, it could also be nuclear weapons, dirty bombs, GPS guided explosive drones and only heaven knows what else is out there that could destroy humankind. Interesting that today the world has the weapons necessary to destroy itself or kill billions of people in a short period of time. All this 'technological advancement' happening in the last 70 -80 years or .13 % of recorded history. Incredible.

Coincidence or fulfilled prophecy?

Revelation 6:8, 9:15

NATURAL DISASTERS…

Horrific natural disaster information and viewing seem to now be a part of our daily lives: fires, floods, earthquakes, massive tornados, hurricanes, record high temperatures, and other earthshattering events that people cannot control, events that very negatively affect people's lives. One of the national 5:30 news outlets now has a daily national weather report because evidently weather (at least in the USA) has frequent adverse effects upon millions of people, virtually every day. I will go out on a limb and say that the words of Jesus re 'earthquakes' would likely, in today's world, be described as 'natural disasters'. The cost of these weather related natural disasters in the USA during 2020 was $306 billion…staggering. The increase in the 'bad weather' is now considered by many the result of greenhouse gasses and they have supposedly come because of the increased emissions which are the result of the increase in 'going to and fro'…isn't that interesting. Whatever the reason, it seems obvious that natural disasters are here to stay and they are a recent phenom on as well. Jesus was so dead on! If you would like to be further informed about daily world weather events, go to: thetwopreachers.com.

Matthew 24:7
Luke 21:25

THIS GOSPEL OF THE KINGDOM WILL BE PREACHED IN ALL THE WORLD...AND THE END SHALL COME

In times past, who could have ever conceived what this meant or how such a thing would ever be possible? Before the printing press, the radio, short wave, television, VCR, computers, batteries, recorders, DVD, solar power, airplanes, or powered ships, Bible translations and missionary efforts were slow and tedious to say the least. Today, because of the advances mentioned above, virtually every portion of the earth, every tribe, nearly every tongue has heard the message of the Good News of Jesus Christ. The missionary movement began about 1750 with missionaries leaving the USA and England, many for the remainder of their life, usually one way tickets. The missionary and translation efforts continue today, except the electronic applications, the modernization of cultures and swift travel have overwhelmed and positively changed the 'difficultly' of the translation and missionary efforts. The result: this prophecy of the 'Gospel to the whole world' is fulfilled in our midst, virtually to the uttermost.

Before we leave this subject, let's take a look at how technology has allowed just one Christian ministry to be involved in the fulfillment of this 'wild' prophetic statement. A ministry called Campus Crusade for Christ (now CRU), some 35 years ago, made a movie depicting the Gospel of Luke and took the film to the 'world'. Here are some stats regarding that movie:

> It has been translated into 1600 languages
>
> It has had 3 billion (one estimate was 7 billion) viewings
>
> It is the most watched movie in film history

There are many ministries that have and continue to bring the Gospel to the world through many various venues. About 8 years ago I was a part of a teaching ministry (30 people) that traveled to Honduras. On the plane traveling back to the States there were three different Christian ministry groups present, all who had been involved in bringing the Gospel to the world in various ways. This is just one example of worldwide movements to fulfill this prophesy.

The statement that when the Gospel is preached in all the world and then The End Shall come… should we not contemplate how close the Gospel is to reaching all of the world, as Jesus said… and then the next major event in God's Great Plan…The Rapture?

Matthew 24:14

MORAL REVOLUTION, WOE TO THE DAYS WHEN EVIL SHALL BE CALLED GOOD AND GOOD EVIL …

We live in a time of the near complete destruction of all traditional, historical, and internationally agreed ethics and morality (Biblical World View). One does not have to be that old to have witnessed the complete undoing of the Biblical view of morals and ethics. We have witnessed the absolute fulfillment of Isaiah 5:20 wherein he said: 'Woe to the days when evil shall be called good and good evil, who put darkness for light and light for darkness, who put bitter for sweet and sweet for bitter'. A classic example of upside down good and evil is the revelation of the rainbow. God established that the rainbow would be an everlasting sign (a covenant from God to all living creatures) that never again would He allow all flesh to be cut off by the waters of such a flood. Now, here we are today dealing with the reality that the symbol of the rainbow is the international flag of homosexuality or gay pride…a complete unearthing of God's intended message. We live in the midst of a complete moral, ethical, and reason (commonsense) revolution, where things are completely upside down when compared to only a few years or decades ago. Multicultural relativism has gradually changed the attitudes of humankind regarding moral and ethical standards, to degrees that I am not sure we even fully understand. Things changed by shades of gray, and they were changing right before our eyes and most did not see it until things became 'very dark'. We now suffer under the weight of political correctness, governmental overreach, and the deconstruction of civil society. As a result, homosexuality is now a part of the normal, gay rights are upheld, gay parades are a part of celebrations, gay couples adopt children, marriage is now redefined to whatever or whomever one would want to marry, and one's sexual orientation is a matter of choice and an operation. We are told that we no longer can use gender specific pronouns, and that it is OK for a 6'3" boy who has decided he is a girl, to now play on a girl's basketball team. We're advised that there are 60 or more ways to identify one's sexual orientation, that Woke is the way, and that LGBTQXYZ, and Progressives have the floor.

Sex before marriage is assumed in most cases, abortion now is into millions of babies each year, and crime is a matter of fact everywhere, and redefined so there is far less penalty than before (California: a theft has to have a value of $950 before it is considered a misdemeanor). Moral and ethical behavior is no longer understood in the simple and narrow ways in which it was intended, like: 'thou shall not', which is easy to say, easy to understand and simple to follow……. The Biblical World View in the recent past was the way by which persons made decisions, whether they were Christians or not…. In today's world that Biblical World View controls fewer and fewer of us and as a result we experience a world without a moral or ethical compass or commonsense and the consequences, as we are experiencing, are overwhelming. Things are now almost completely 'upside down'… the definition of a revolution. In the recent past, most people of the world knew little or nothing of these truly upside-down cultural changing moral and ethical revolutionary issues. Not so today.

TAKE HEED THAT NO ONE DECEIVES YOU…

In Mathew 24 the disciples asked Jesus what the times will be like at the time of His return and the End of the Age. The very 1st thing Jesus responded with was the warning about 'Deception'. One verse later He warns of deception again and then 6 verses later he says it once more. Do we not live in a time when one does not know what to believe, whether what one has read or heard is in fact the truth. It is assumed in some circles, that lying is simply a part of the language (politics, news networks, business, government). Stretching the truth for advantage is lying and certainly a part of modern story telling. A survey regarding one national news network revealed that about 85% of those that watched, believed that they were being lied to. Integrity it seems, has flown the coop.

Lying is one thing, an intentional violation of truth. Deception is yet a grander more deliberate betrayal of the truth with greater consequences to the one being deceived. Deception implies deliberate misrepresentation of facts so the individual or society accepts what is false as truth… the breaking of faith while appearing to be loyal. These are the scenarios that Jesus said would be prevalent at the Time of His Coming and The End of the Age. What is so difficult today is to know when to believe that what is being told is in fact the truth.

Why is it so difficult today for folks on the opposite sides of the 'isle' to get along, to come to common ground, or to try to understand each other? Could it be that at least a part of the problem is that the two parties cannot agree on what is true and therefore the very language fails to communicate properly…words have no meaning common to both sides. This then becomes an avenue to even more insidious consequences.

Matthew 24:3-5, 11

ARE WE RUNNING OUT OF TIME?...

The start of the End Times Prophecy Calendar began on May 14, 1948 when Israel was declared a sovereign nation by the United Nations. Jesus referred to the Nation of Israel in Matthew 24:32, as a fig tree in its beginning. Jesus was now talking to the Church and said that all of the prophecies that He and the other prophets had proclaimed, would be dated, tied to the rebirth of the Nation of Israel and would be fulfilled in one generation from the birth of the Nation of Israel… a Biblical generation is referred to as 70 or perhaps 80 years. In the context of the Matthew Chapter 24 Olivet Discourse conversation with His inner circle, Jesus was asked three straight forward questions and in response Jesus then gave straight forward answers. The answers were not intended to weave a theological puzzle. The answers that Jesus gave, simply interpreted, are that from 1948 to the end of the prophetic completion period it would be 2018 for 70 years or 2028 for 80 years. Based upon this truth, the reality is that, in the context of time, we are very near the end of the prophetic time period of the Rapture of the church and the beginning of the Tribulation Period. 'Glory days for the believers and gloomy days for those Left Behind'. The above is a catchy little phrase, but the extremes between glory and gloomy in this context cannot be put into words or even imagination.

Matthew 24:34

THE WAR OF GOG AND MAGOG…

The war of Gog and Magog is a future war where Russia and several of its Muslim allies will invade Israel to take plunder and because Israel will be so vulnerable, outnumbered & alone (without allies), that the God of the Bible will step in and literally destroy the invading armies. According to Ezekiel, 5/6 of the Russian and allied armies will be destroyed and it will take Israel 7 months to bury the dead and 7 years for Israel to deal with the rubble left behind. The war takes place just before the Rapture… or just after the Tribulation Period begins (theologians are not in agreement). The details are explained in Ezekiel Chapters 36-39. Is it just coincidental that Russia is once again referred to as Russia (Rosh in the Ezekiel passage refers to Russia) where in the recent past Russia was referred to as the USSR or the Soviet Union? What are we to think regarding Russia's evil pursuit of the Ukrainian nation and no one seems to effectively resist their evil destruction? How will that Russian invasion change the world in every way imaginable? Any applications to the future? Also, the invading allied nations that are referenced in Ezekiel Chapter 38 were nations when Ezekiel was written (2700 years ago) and are still identifiable nations today. That alone is quite remarkable. Those nations are Israel, Russia, Iran, Ethiopia, Libya, Sudan, & the territory of Eastern Europe.

Ezekiel Chapters 36-39

FOR THE TIME WILL COME WHEN THEY WILL NOT PUT UP WITH SOUND DOCTRINE……THE SPIRIT EXPRESSLY SAYS THAT IN THE LATTER TIMES, SOME WILL DEPART FROM THE FAITH…

'The Faith' as expressed by the Apostle Paul is the 'faith' that can be assured by the Word of God and further supported by the doctrines and creeds of the Christian Church such as the Apostles Creed, the Nicene Creed, and others. In contrast, an individual can create his own 'faith' based upon personal opinions or experiences plus the Bible and the result is an error-based faith when compared to faith as described in the Bible and supported by careful examination. Examples would be:

- Pentecostal extremism
- Liberalism-deny supernatural
- Legalism
- TV evangelists….select 'easy believeism'
- Replacement Theology
- Dominion Theology

Many recent books, videos, movies, and programs that deny and distort Biblical truth and doctrine

All of the above are recent departures from Biblical Faith, some within the last 50 years. The Christian Church is challenged on many fronts to remain pure to the Word and the supporting doctrines and statements of faith. The challenge for the Church and those that make up the Church are the words of Jesus "When the Son of Man returns, will he really find faith on the Earth."

Charles Spurgeon is credited with the following wisdom: Discernment is not knowing the difference between right and wrong, it is knowing the difference between right and almost right.

I Tim. 4:1-2
II Tim. 3:13-14
II Tim. 4:1-5
I John 4:1-3

GLOBALISM, A ONE WORLD GOVERNMENT CONTROLLING VIRTUALLY EVERYONE AND EVERYTHING…

Globalism was an unknown description and understanding not many years ago. Today it is a part of the Progressive conversation and would include all of the following titles and objectives:

New World Order, One World Order
One World Government, Economy & Global Currency
The end of National sovereignty
Microchip citizens/mandatory vaccines
Progressive
Universal basic income
End of fossil fuels/renewal energy
Open borders
World Central Bank
Population goals of 1 billion people or less
Woke
CRT
BLM
World Economic Forum

This is a part of many conversations and interests today and seemingly the reality of the world of tomorrow. This one world government is described in the prophesy of Revelation Chapter 13. 2000 years ago the descriptions of the world to come were penned by many writers of the New Testament and today those Globalists descriptions appear to be in the late stages of becoming a reality, during our modern era time in history.

Again, a read of Revelation 13 will be quite revealing regarding soon coming events and changes that we can foresee because of what has already been going on…and then realize that these insights were written 2000 years ago.

Revelation Chapter 13

SHEMITAH CYCLE AND THE 7000 YEARS OF EARTHLY HISTORY…

If you are up to studying it, here is a definitive picture of how God records history and more specifically where we might be, date wise, in relation to the beginning of the 7 Year Tribulation Period. The Tribulation takes place shortly after the Rapture of the Church and starts with a treaty between the Nation of Israel and the world leader (the Antichrist). Some supporters of Shemitah (a 7 year Sabbatical cycle) believe that at the end of the present Shemitah 7 year period, it will be the beginning of the Tribulation Period. A very interesting study to say the least. Some scholars and supporters of Shemitah make a further claim that the beginning of the Tribulation period could be quite soon and therefore the Rapture before that. This study is too much to take on in this writing, and is somewhat controversial in that it is understood by so few… but is likely a further revelation that we live in the closing era of recorded history.

IN CONCLUSION…

What do you think? The evidence is overwhelming…. that seems obvious. At the closing of the Apostle Paul's life, only hours before he was executed, Paul wrote chapter 4 of II Timothy. His concluding challenge to his readers is evidence of his opinion regarding the 'Soon and Very Soon' return of Jesus Christ. In vs 8 Paul pens this: "Finally, there is laid up for me the Crown of Righteousness, which the Lord, the Righteous Judge will give to me on that day, and not to me only, but also to all who have longed for His appearing". The return of Jesus Christ for His Church was a major theme of Paul's ministry, up to the very last moments of his life. Should we not be like minded with the Great Apostle regarding his thoughts about the Savior of the World and His coming back again to rescue from the Earth those who 'believe'? According to Paul, the folks living during the Time of the End or the Last Days will either be a part of those Raptured to Heaven, (Soon and Very Soon), or will be a part of the millions 'Left Behind' to experience the ravages of the 7 year Tribulation Period. It is really that clear!!!

Some of us can remember the pictures of the closing hours of the War in Vietnam, from the rooftop of the US Embassy in Saigon. Helicopters were going to and from the rooftop rescuing those who desperately did not want to, and could not bear the thought of being Left Behind. The chaos of that event was because there was a way to be rescued and there were those who recognized their opportunity was 'now'. The evacuees knew this was their opportunity and did anything to be on that chopper.

More recently a similar senario took place in Afghanistan where American C-17 Globemaster airplanes were loaded (standing room only) with volumes of people. Americans and Afghans who could not bear the thought of being Left Behind in Afghanistan scrambled to be on one of those airplanes. The thought of surviving in Afghanistan in the absence of the US military was unthinkable, and therefore the mad desperate push to be on board. Similarly, each of us should have a 'like' attitude and come to faith in Jesus Christ in order to have the blessings of Heaven and avoid the ravages of the coming Tribulation Period.

As the world faces continual crises, and as evil flourishes everywhere, you can yet have the assurance that you are secure in the hands of Almighty God. Come to Jesus Christ today and be saved. You must turn away from sin and trust Jesus as your Lord and Savior. If you will do that, God promises to give you a new beginning and a new life that is both abundant and eternal. Right now, where ever you are, you can begin a relationship with God. It is the most important thing you will ever do. Start by simply talking to God. Pray a prayer like this: "Dear God, I know that I am a sinner. I am sorry for my sin. I want to turn from my sin. Please forgive me. I believe Jesus is your Son; I believe He died on a cross for my sin and that You raised Him from the dead. I want Him to come into my heart and take control of my life. I want to trust Jesus as my Savior and follow Him as Lord of my life from this day forward. In Jesus name, Amen."

We wait for Jesus to rescue us from the wrath to come and to give us eternal life by believing in Him as written to us in the Bible.

The Apostle Paul gave us this great reminder, in fact there are two to consider:

1. In I Thessalonians 1:10. Paul put it specifically like this: To wait for His Son from Heaven, whom He raised from the dead, Jesus, who rescues us from the coming wrath.
2. Then Paul wrote Romans 10:9-10 that says this: That if you confess with your mouth that Jesus is Lord, and believe in your heart that God raised Him from the dead, you will be saved. For it is with your heart that you believe and are justified, and it is with your mouth that you confess and are saved.

How is it that we can be rescued and saved for eternity if we neglect to grasp such a Great Salvation? The answer is that we cannot. Now is the time of Salvation…tomorrow could be too late.

I Thessalonians 1:10
Romans 10:9-10

OUR HOPE....

For the grace of God that brings salvation has appeared to all men, teaching us that, denying ungodliness and worldly lusts, we should live soberly, righteously, and godly in the present age, looking for the blessed hope and glorious appearing of our great God and Savior Jesus Christ, who gave Himself for us that He might redeem us from every lawless deed and purify for Himself His own special people, zealous for good works.

Titus 2:11-14